Prince of the Fairway:
The Tiger Woods Story

Allison L. Teague

PRINCE OF THE FAIRWAY:
THE TIGER WOODS STORY

ALLISON L. TEAGUE

AVISSON PRESS, INC.
GREENSBORO

First Edition.
Printed in the United States of America.

Library of Congress Cataloging-in-Publication Data

Teague, Allison L., 1964-
   Prince of the Fairway: the Tiger Woods story/Allison
   L. Teague. — 1st ed.
      p.   cm..— (Avisson young adult series)
   Includes bibliographical references (p.) and index.
   Summary: Describes the life and accomplishments of the racially mixed golfer who became the youngest winner of the Masters Tournament.
   ISBN 1-888105-22-4 (lib. bdg.)
   1. Woods, Tiger—Juvenile literature. 2. Golfers—United States—Biography—Juvenile literature. [1. Woods, Tiger. 2. Golfers. 3. Racially mixed people—Biography.] I. Title. II. Series. GB964.W66T43 1997
796.352'092—dc21
[B]   97-24122
                                                      CIP
                              AC

Frontispiece: AP/Wide World Photos

Dedication:
*To Our Daughter,
Mary Catherine*

CONTENTS

"WUNDERKIND"

THE YOUNG GOLFER who sat dejectedly in the locker room at the Augusta National Country Club that day in April, 1995 should, by ordinary standards, have felt proud rather than disappointed. The tournament was half over. Though his score was far from the leaders, he had accomplished much during the past week.

He was the youngest player ever invited to compete at the Masters, golf's most prestigious tournament. As reigning U.S. Amateur champion, he had been given a suite of rooms over the club house which looked out on the historic course; he merely had to walk out the door to take practice shots on the driving range. In practice rounds that week, he had played with golfing legends such as Raymond Floyd, Greg Norman, and Gary Player. He had shot a first round 72, par on the tough course, and four strokes better than golfing greats Jack Nicklaus and Arnold Palmer had done in their first tournament rounds there. After a solid second round, he had made the "Cut," as it is called—his score in the first half of the tournament was better than many veteran pros, who now had to drop out and go home.

But he was Tiger Woods, the young superstar of amateur golf, the prodigy, the golfing genius who was supposed to win all the time. Even against men who were twice his age, pros like Greg Norman, Fred Couples, Jay Haas, Davis Love III—seasoned professionals who were acknowledged masters of the game—he was supposed to win. And he hadn't.

It would have been only human for him to look back at past accomplishments, the titles and trophies he had already won in his short life. And they were many. He was three-time National Amateur Champion. Before that, he had been three-time National Junior Amateur Champion. Both feats were not likely to be equalled. In fact, he had only lost three times in match-play (one-on-one) competition. Such were his skills that he was already something of a golfing legend.

At least there was something to do to help his disappointment, though it still, as most everything in his life, involved golf. Later that afternoon, he accompanied his father Earl to a public course in the 'black' section of Augusta, where he put on a clinic for young golfers. Many in the African-American community there showed up, congratulating him for the things he had already done, and showing confidence that he would do even greater things in the future, both as a golfer and as a 'minority' golfer. His great talent would break barriers in the historically all-white world of professional golf, and most especially the world of the great championships, the Masters and the U.S. Open. Neither had ever been won by a person of color.

Golfing fans had been waiting impatiently for this prince of the fairway to turn professional, and to compete against the very best players in the world of professional golf, to try to better the records of men of legendary skill such as Nicklaus and Palmer. Armed with a skill and playing poise beyond his years, the youthful prodigy was expected to continue his path to glory.

But, as Tiger Woods went to sleep that night, he knew those things would have to wait, at least for a while. He was, after all, only 19 years of age.

The next day, Tiger did not play well, and shot a 77, which put him out of contention for the championship. After a long conference with his dad, he decided that his problem that day had been hitting the ball too strongly on his approach shots to the green. A decision was made that he should use a different set of irons borrowed from his coach

Butch Harmon, to compensate for the strength of his swing. After additional practice with the new clubs, he felt some of his confidence return.

On Sunday, Woods shot an even-par 72. This was not a spectacular round; but perhaps Tiger was beginning to get the hang of the tough Augusta course. He finished strongly, with birdies on three of the last four holes. His total score put him at 41st place in the standings. But he had been the only amateur to make the cut; automatically, he was "low amateur" for the Masters, a notable achievement in itself.

So, he had done well, much better than a teenager had a right to expect in such august company. But, as he headed back to California and the university where he was a student, he must have thought to himself, *I will be back. And the next time, I will win.*

Eldrick "Tiger" Woods was literally trained, from infancy, to be the greatest golfer the world has ever known. His parents, Earl and Kutilda "Tida" Woods, had made sure of that. Earl and Tida had always been been the guiding force behind this vibrant young star of the sports world. Earl, a former Army lieutenant colonel of the famous

Green Beret commandos, had molded his son into a young man with the potential for golfing greatness. Tida, a former Army secretary and native of Thailand, had always been a second powerful force, a loving mother but one with a firm hand who served as a model of discipline for Tiger.

Earl and Tida met in the late 1960's in Bangkok, Thailand, the Southeast Asian country where Earl was based as a soldier. His previous years of military experience during the Vietnam War in the mid-1960's had made him an invaluable military asset to his country. During two full tours of duty, Earl had endured and survived many dangerous, even deadly, missions behind enemy lines. The Vietnam War had created bitter political and social divisions among Americans, but also produced some of the most unlikely friendships. Earl and Tida would soon discover that love is universal, and has no geographical or cultural boundaries.

In many ways, the couple were complete opposites. Earl was 37, with one marriage behind him, while Tida was a much younger, never-married 23. He was one-quarter American Indian, one-quarter Chinese, and half African-American. She was half-Thai, one-quarter Chinese, and one-quarter Caucasian. Earl had been raised in the small, rural town of Manhattan, Kansas, while Tida lived in the exotic, big city of Bangkok. Earl was a professional soldier with two tours of duty in Vietnam and one in Thailand, while Tida was a peaceful civilian. He was Protestant and she was Buddhist. Earl had pretty much raised himself when, at the age of 13, both his parents had died. Tida was from a wealthy family and still lived with her parents.

It did not seem as if a romance could even get started, let alone lead to marriage.

It was difficult enough for the couple to go out together on a date. The clash of different cultures immediately led to a misunderstanding. When Earl asked Tida to meet him for the date at 8:00, he assumed they would meet at 8:00 in the evening. But she meant 8:00 in the *morning*. Earl did not realize that in Thailand the women do not go out on dates unchaperoned, and certainly not after dark. "Thai girls not go out at night," Tida would recall proudly. That night, Earl grew weary waiting for Tida to show up for their date, and went back to his quarters alone. He thought he had been stood up. Disappointed with the evening, he went to sleep early.

As the new day began, Earl heard a knocking on his door. Tida and her girlfriend stood anxiously in the doorway, looking slightly puzzled. "We had a date," Tida said. Earl tried his best to explain what had happened the night before, but Tida was still confused. After they talked, Tida informed Earl that it was a holy day in Bangkok and she wanted him to escort her to the Temple of the Reclining Buddha.

"We still have a date," Tida remembered, and smiled sweetly at Earl.

"What could I do?" Earl later recalled. The reunited couple strolled to the Temple of the Reclining Buddha with their chaperone close behind.

In spite of such an inauspicious start, the romance did blossom, and it was not long before the two realized they were in love.

Earl and Tida were married in 1969 and moved to Brooklyn, New York. Later they relocated to Cypress, California, a pleasant town which is 35 miles southeast of Los Angeles. The Woods both dreamed of having a child, and on December 30th, 1975, their son Eldrick "Tiger" Woods was born.

Earl and Tida created the name Eldrick from a combination of their own names, but the name "Tiger" was of another origin. While Earl was in Vietnam he had fought beside a South Vietnamese soldier named Nguyen Phong. Nguyen Phong was

Earl's close friend. Earl nicknamed him "Tiger" because of his fearless bravery on their many missions together. As Earl later related to *Sports Illustrated*, it was Tiger who led him on a dangerous mission through the streets of an enemy-held village, an action which won for him the Vietnamese Silver Star. It was Tiger, his best friend, who on another mission pulled him off a rice-paddy dike while sniper fire tore over them.

The two battle-weary friends had lost touch with one another in 1967. But Earl believes that his buddy is still alive and hopes that he will hear about his famous son, the golfer, and know that he had honored Phong by naming him Tiger.

Tida suffered complications during childbirth, and learned sadly that she could never have more children. In Asia, the first-born son is considered to be the most important child, because one day he will be responsible for the family financially and make decisions when his parents grow old. Earl and Tida thus decided to channel all their love and energy into their one and only child. They would work constantly to help him to be strong and successful. Both parents' love was strong, but each had differing roles to play in Tiger's life. As Tiger grew up, Earl became as much a best friend as a father, while Tida would handle much of the discipline, and be the one to spank him when necessary. In later years on the golf tour, Earl would accompany the golfing genius all over the world, a combination of companion, father, and teacher. Tida usually stayed behind to manage the house, waiting and worrying while they were away from home.

Tiger seemed to be born to play golf. When he was a baby barely able to walk, he began to watch Earl practice hitting golf balls into a net in the garage of their suburban home. The child was so fascinated by this that Tida moved his highchair into the garage and began to feed him there while Earl hit his practice shots. Earl began to teach Tiger the game. Earl shortened a putter for little Tiger, and soon he was putting into the net. As Earl later told *Golf* magazine, "He waggled like I did, looked at the net, and pulled the trigger. Then he was hitting it left-handed. But in a couple of weeks, in the middle of hitting some balls, he just turned around and got on the other side of the ball. He was hitting on target, squaring up the clubface."[1]

By any measure, Tiger was not an ordinary toddler. He was an enthusiastic golfer when he could barely stand up. His Mom and Dad would take him to the nearby Navy golf course, only a short drive from their home. Tiny Tiger would practice hitting golf balls; Tida would then have to put him back into his baby stroller and give him his bottle.

By the age of two, Tiger was commenting on adult golfers' swings. "Look daddy, he has a reverse pivot!" the child might say while watching an adult. Earl recalls how Tiger was looking at some sequence photographs of his swing and understood the need to make certain changes in it. That same year, Tiger began competing, always against much older youngsters, and won his first competition, at a pitch-and-putt course in Cypress. At the age of three, he was already beating ten-year-olds, and shot a score of 48 for nine holes, a better showing than many adults could make. This was so odd that it made a good news story. The tiny athlete was asked to be a guest on the popular "Mike Douglas Show," where he competed in a putting contest with the famous comedian and amateur golfer Bob Hope (and won).

At four, Earl took Tiger and entered him into his first golf tournament. Many people would say that Earl was insisting on too much from his son at such an early age. But Tiger has never felt that way; he has often said, "Pop is my best friend." A later coach for Woods remarked, "So far as I know, Earl never pushed Tiger to do anything." The reverse was often the case: it was difficult to get a golf club out of Tiger's hands.

At four, little Tiger was signing autographs in block letters because he could not yet write in script.

The Woods were fortunate to live in the warm, golf-loving Southern California area while Tiger was growing up; the lad was able at the age of four to join the Southern California Junior Golf Association of Heartwell Golf Park in Long Beach. He competed in the ten-and-under age bracket with no handicap against competitors far older than himself. The organization (SCJGA) sponsored one-day tournaments during the summer months four or five times a week at some of the most exclusive country clubs. "This fit perfectly into my master game plan for Tiger to grow up and develop on the highest caliber golf courses,"[2] Earl recalled. The elder Woods already saw that his son could be a prodigy. Tiger once said that his first memory of golf was when he brought home a big trophy from a local junior tournament, at age four. This must have been when Tiger won his first nine-hole competition at the Yorba Linda Country Club, beating many ten-year-olds, and was overjoyed at the victory.

Earl Woods writes in his recent book, *Training A Tiger: A Father's Guide to Raising a Winner in Both Golf and Life*: "When Tiger was four, I realized that he was so talented that he needed the services of a professional to accelerate his development. So I turned him over to Rudy Duran, the head pro at Heartwell Golf Park. Rudy was an affable former PGA Tour player who had a reputation as an excellent teacher with a devout interest in junior golf. Paramount in the selection of Tiger's mentor was my decision to stand in the background and let the two develop a working relationship. Support is much more productive than interference."[3]

By age five, Tiger was competing in local junior competitions against 17-year-olds, and again appeared on television, this time as a featured guest on the popular television show, "That's Incredible". Newspaper, magazine and television reporters began showing up at the Woods' comfortable home in Cypress. They all wanted to interview and write about this wondrous youngster.

When Tiger was six, he began to listen to a 'subliminal' tape. Subliminal tapes are recordings used to let the 'subconscious' mind absorb messages which will change the listener's attitudes and help self-confidence in daily activities. Positive messages are spoken from the tape, but at a lower volume than music or other sounds which are clearly heard. While listening to the subliminal tapes, the listener is unaware of how the subconscious mind is to be 'programmed', but will begin to exhibit those qualities afterwards. Medical authorities have great doubts as to whether such tapes have real value, but in Tiger's case the masked messages may have helped turn his young mind into a powerhouse of concentration and determination. Underneath the sounds of trickling brooks and lilting flute melodies were messages such as MY DECISIONS ARE STRONG! I DO IT ALL WITH MY HEART!

Tiger enjoyed listening to the tapes, and understood what they were for. As a first-grader, he would use them while he practiced his swing in front of the mirror, or watched videos of old Masters golf tournaments, the most prestigious of all championships. His tiny room was filled with printed posters of the subliminal messages of the tapes. He had tacked them all along his bookshelves as a constant reminder of their power.

With such dedication, Tiger's game continued to improve. It was not long before he had his first hole-in-one; soon after, he stroked another.

His father began to train Tiger psychologically when his son was seven. Earl knew a little about 'psychological warfare' from his 20 years in the military, and used this knowledge to help his son. Earl tried everything he could think of to distract, ruffle and otherwise annoy him while he played. He might jingle keys while Tiger was trying to putt, or mark a higher score on the scorecard than Tiger had actually made. He was trying to rattle his son, or make him angry, so that Tiger would have to focus on his game no matter what the distractions and, as a soldier would, "complete his mission" regardless of the conditions around him. Tiger understood that the new training was for his benefit, and accepted all the antics his dad could dish out. Before tournaments, Earl would ask him to check his equipment and be sure it was in "tip-top shape, lie and loft." Earl made sure his son understood the 'mission' (to win), and would hold 'debriefings' afterward to discuss the game, in the same way that a soldier would make a report to his superiors after going on a dangerous combat mission. Tiger toughened up emotionally, and it seemed as if a different, almost icy personality took over whenever he was on the golf course. He learned not to flinch at anything. Tiger couldn't hear a word as he was poised at the tee. The subliminal messages, now meshed with his psychological training, had made him into a fierce opponent.

Tiger Woods had become a nationally recognized name while he was still in the second grade. That year, he competed in and won several junior tournaments. But in some respects, the wonder boy was like other kids his age. Watching television shows such as 'The Simpsons', and going to the local mall to hang out, were among his favorite things to do. He was a dutiful student whose grades at school were well above average. The only obvious difference from most other kids was his poor vision; he was wearing thick glasses by age nine or ten. Later, he would get contact lenses to correct the problem.

Tiger's dicipline at home helped him strive to be the best he could be in all things. Of course, he did get into trouble sometimes, but he was a good kid and knew his parents wanted only the best for him. He respected that, and tried to do the right thing for their sake as well as his own.

At age eight, young Woods won the Optimist International Junior World Tournament, one of the first of half a dozen wins in this championship.

When Tiger was ten, his teaching pro Rudy Duran took a new position at the Chalk Mountain Golf Club in Atescadero, California, leaving an uncomfortable void in the young man's life. Earl conducted an extensive search for the best teaching pro available, and soon found John Anselmo. Anselmo was the head teaching pro at Meadowlark Golf Course in Huntington Beach, California. The veteran pro was hired to mentor the young athlete.

As had just about everyone who had seen Woods, the new coach felt Tiger was capable of anything on the golf course. Anselmo commented to *Golf* magazine at the time: "He [Tiger] is a mature player, but I have to remember that he is still a boy, and I try to keep it fun for him. He's a pure swinger like a Tom Purtzer, and he has touch and reflexes you can't teach."[4] Anselmo also compared Tiger's swing to that of Teddy Rhodes, a wonderful black professional golfer who played in the 1940's and 50's.

With Anselmo's guidance, the Woods legend continued to grow as Tiger, at age eleven, went undefeated in Southern California junior golf events, some 30 tournaments in all. Each event had at least 100 competitors. His trophy room was overflowing with evidence of his athletic prowess.

When Tiger was twelve, he was still undefeated and was ready for a new level of competition. Earl decided to enter his son in his first national competition. But the elder Woods let Tiger choose the tournament in which he wanted to play. He chose the Big I (Independent Insurance Agents of America Golf Tournament) held in Texarkana, Arkansas. "The choice to allow him to advance to the national level was easy for me because Tiger had clearly demonstrated his superiority over local talent in his age group,"[18] Earl writes in *Training A Tiger*. "This tournament has a unique format in that after the thirty-six-hole cut, they bring in PGA tour players to match up with three competitors to enable them to play a round of golf with a pro. At thirteen, Tiger's pro was John Daly, then an unknown . . . On this day the pros played from the same tees as the competitors and, with four holes to play, Tiger was two strokes ahead of John."[5]

But this was one afternoon when Tiger had met his match. Earl continued his tale: "I distinctly remember John saying to all who would listen, I cannot let a thirteen-year-old beat me. And he didn't. He birdied three of the last four holes to defeat Tiger by one stroke. Today, Tiger and John are very good friends. And I have seen them laugh and joke and tell others about that humid, torrid day in Texarkana."[6]

Earl Woods added sports psychologist and Navy Captain Jay Brunza to what would later be called "Team Tiger" when the young golfer was 13. Brunza was an old family friend. Tiger was completely open to improvement through a new form of psychological training, that of hypnosis. And he proved to be a good subject; Brunza was able to hypnotize him in under one minute. While under hypnosis, a person's consciousness narrows and they are in a state very similar to a dream or a trance. The hypnotist then can make suggestions that the "subject" either be more relaxed or more confident during stressful situations—for example, when trying to win a golf match.

After one of the first sessions, Brunza asked Tiger to play golf with a group of his friends. One of the men came back grumbling and said, "What kind of monster have you created? He's birdied five of the first seven holes!"

Once, in an experiment, Brunza put Woods under a hypnotic trance and said, "Tiger, hold your arm out straight." And he did. "Now, Earl, try to bend it," the hypnotist asked his father. Earl attempted to pull, push and bend his arm. He even hung his full weight from the arm, but Tiger didn't flinch once, the level of his hypnotic concentration was so deep.

Soon Tiger was so proficient at this new training method that he was able to hypnotize himself whenever he felt the need. In some cases, he played under such strong self-hypnosis that he could make an amazing shot and not even remember hitting it, although he could recall the club he had used.

By age 13, Tiger had already shot five holes-in-one. He also had engaged in an exhibition match with legendary old-time golfer "Slammin'" Sam

Snead. A year later, at age 14, Woods became the youngest player ever to win the Insurance Youth Golf Classic. In that same year he won the Junior World title for the fifth time. His achievements included being runner-up in the PGA National Junior Championship; semi-finalist in the USGA Junior Championship; and being named as Southern California Junior Player of the Year.

Woods said at that time: "I want to be the next dominant player. I want to go to college, turn pro, and tear it up on tour. I want to win more majors than anybody ever has."[7]

When Tiger turned 16, Earl enlisted the PGA Tour swing coach Claude "Butch" Harmon, Jr. of Houston to refine his son's skill. Harmon is the son of 1948 Masters champion Claude Harmon.

Tiger was an eager student, to say the least. "He wants to work with me 24 hours a day," Harmon declared. "I can't get him off the phone." Harmon also commented that "he handles pressure like a 30-year-old. And his creativity is amazing. Some of the shots I've seen him hit remind me of Greg Norman and Arnold Palmer."

Under the tutelage of the new coach, Tiger was the youngest player ever invited to participate in a Professional Golfers Association (PGA) tour event, the Nissan Los Angeles Open in 1992. He was only

16 years, 2 months old. He was still very much an amateur golfer, but already people were beginning to ask: When will Tiger turn professional?

Young Man With A Mission

TIGER WOODS CONFIDENTLY strolled the greens at the 1993 U.S. Junior Amateur in Portland, Oregon. He wanted badly to tie the record of his idol, Jack Nicklaus, by the end of the day by winning his third U.S. Junior Amateur Championship. But Tiger, now 17, would have to defeat Ryan Armour, 16, of Silver Lake, Ohio. Armour was a tough competitor who had matured greatly from the previous year when Tiger walked away with his 2nd U.S. Amateur Championship. And, Woods was recovering from a bout with mononucleosis just three weeks previous. Armour and Woods were tied on the par-3 9th hole, and again on 15. On the 16th, Tiger's four-foot putt for par lipped out.

Armour later told *Sports Illustrated*, "I thought, two pars and the national title is yours." And he was very close to the win; but a Tiger was lurking nearby. Woods had become famous for his comebacks. On a 432-yard, par-4 17th he came roaring back with a nine-iron shot that came within eight feet of the pin. Tiger knew that if he missed the next putt it would finish him. Tiger whispered to Jay Brunza, his caddie and sports psychologist: "Got to be like Nicklaus. Got to *will* this in the hole." Laserlike concentration moved the ball to the cup to pull him within one stroke. Earl was anxiously waiting to see what the next play would bring. The 578-yard, par-5 18th would be very exciting as Tiger rocketed his drive more than 300 yards. As father Earl recounted for *Sports Illustrated*, "After he airmailed it, he turned around and saw Armour pull out an iron, and Tiger's face hardened. Tiger realized Armour was just trying to make par, and he said to himself, You think I can't birdie this hole? I'll show you what I got."[8]

It was a risky shot, and Woods's three-iron from the rough disappeared into a bunker 40 yards from the green. But his next shot was right on target. Opponent Armour later said, "I'm thinking, He'll be lucky to get it on the green, and he knocks it to within 10 feet. How good is that?"[9]

Armour only had to worry about a tap-in par, while Tiger would have a tough shot for birdie. He summoned his powers to sink the 10-footer. The gallery cheered wildly as Woods walked off the green.

"Sudden death" on the first hole, a 333- yard par-4, would be the battleground for the championship. Tiger launched his second shot to land within 20 feet of the cup. Armour joined Woods on the green, but 60 feet from the hole. Armour missed a slippery downhill seven-foot comebacker and finished in three strokes. Tiger stopped his first putt within four feet and then sank his second putt for the win.

Earl Woods recalled his strong emotion as Tiger rushed to him, saying "I did it, I did it!" The father embraced his son and said to him, "I'm so proud of you, I'm so proud of you." Even the spectators were euphoric as father and son watched another dream come true. As Earl later said, "Time stops in moments like that."

"It was the most amazing comeback of my career," Tiger recalled. " I had to play the best two holes of my life under the toughest circumstances, and I did it."

Besides being an exceptional young golfer, Tiger had matured into a clean-cut, courteous teenager that almost everyone liked. His beaming personality radiated outward to everyone he met. The young golfer certainly seemed as virtuous on the inside as he was proficient on the outside. Tida and Earl had taught him at every opportunity that above all his character and education were worth more than gold. He understood the need to do his homework before he could practice. Earl would shower him with messages such as "Care and Share" and "Expect the best. Prepare for the worst." Tida would be right behind Earl to offer her moral and religious guidance. "Tiger, you pray to Buddha yet?" she might ask. She also taught Tiger about the value of "face", a particularly Asian concept in which great importance is placed on the appearance one makes to other people and to society at large. "Face" sometimes demands that a person keep his or her emotions tightly bottled; it is considered bad form to appear troubled, anxious, frightened, or angry.

Tida explained her concept: "I don't want the one and only [son] to grow up spoiled. So I sit him down by TV one day, watch John McEnroe. [McEnroe is a champion tennis player known for his outbursts of temper on the court.] I tell Tiger, 'See that? Never that. I don't like that. I not have my reputation as parent ruined by that'."[11]

Tida Woods even reported her son to the tournament director when one day Tiger smashed his club on his bag after a bad shot. She demanded that he be penalized two strokes for such behavior.

"Mom!" he said.

"Shut up," she said. "Did club move? Did bag

The two great golfing champions of modern times, Arnold Palmer (standing) and Jack Nicklaus, "The Golden Bear," during a tournament in 1995 (AP/Wide World Photos).

move? Who make bad shot? Whose fault? You want to hit something? Hit yourself in head!"[12]

Tiger was practically born with a golf club in his hand, so quite naturally his swing was highly developed. He had grown up with the game of golf as other kids grow up with baseball or basketball. And Tiger was as physically fit as any player, amateur or professional. He stayed in top shape by putting himself through a daily exercise program which included one hour of weight training, a half hour of aerobics, and another half hour of stretching exercises. His six-foot, 2-inch frame was lean at 148 pounds, but as he matured he could bench press 215 pounds for multiple repititions. Though slender, he was, and would remain, very strong.

As Woods' public visibility grew and his fame spread, two things became obvious. The first was that, barring injury, Tiger was going to be one of the best golfers the world had ever seen. And the second, that he was of mixed race. It was a *real* mixture, with bloodlines from all over the world. But his father was African-American, or mostly African-American. He *looked* African-American, and so did his son. In the United States, this meant that for all practical purposes, Tiger would be seen as and identified as, African-American. And golf is primarily a 'white' or Caucasian sport, at least at the professional level. If his winning ways continued, this would mean increasing controversy.

In the 1940's and 50's many doors were closed

to black athletes, especially golfers. Opportunities to prove themselves were rare. Earl Woods knew this well. He was the first black to play baseball in the Big Eight Conference, at Kansas State University in the late 1940's. Segregation was still in effect, which meant that when the team traveled, Earl could not stay in the same hotel as his teammates. He faced many challenges in what was then a highly racist society.

The situation had been much easier for his son. Tiger knew the barriers he faced were nothing compared to his dad's era, but nevertheless he had felt the numbing shock of racism for himself. The family recalls an incident on Tiger's first day of kindergarten, where Tiger was tied to a tree because he was the only black child at the school.

Other incidents had occurred as well. When they first moved to Cypress, California, Earl and then-pregnant Tida were harassed and frightened by some neighbors. They were the first "black" family to move into the neighborhood. Earl had been a colonel in the Army, and had retired to take a well-paid position as consultant to the McDonnell Douglas Corporation. The neighborhood was solidly middle-class. But the "welcome wagon" for the couple included a barrage of BB-gun pellets which showered their new home, and teenagers throwing fruit at the windows.

All of this must have been very confusing to a young man who has often said: "I don't want to be the best black golfer ever, I want to be the best *golfer* ever."[13] Tiger, when filling out forms, had always put his race as "Asian." But the media and the public soon made defining Tiger's race a national pastime. Tida, who is proud of her Thai heritage, has said, "All the media try to put black in him. Why don't they ask who half of Tiger is from? In United States, one little part black is all black. Nobody want to listen to me. I been trying to explain to people, but they don't understand. To say he is 100 percent black is to deny his heritage. To deny his grandmother and grandfather. To deny *me!*"[14]

Earl is very practical about the matter, and tells Tiger, "When you're in America, be black. When you're in the Orient, be Asian."

For years, Jim Thorpe, 48, had been the only African-American on the PGA tour. He is one of the last of a generation of talented black golfers that includes men such as Lee Elder, Charlie Sifford, Jim Dent, Calvin Peete and Pete Brown. As youngsters they learned the game by working as caddies, carrying clubs around for older golfers. But now, golfers at clountry clubs and some public courses ride around the course in golf carts instead of walking. There are few, if any, jobs as caddies for youngsters, especially those from poor or black families. And the interest in golf had declined as well. Once, Jim Thorpe even went into inner-city neighborhoods and tried to give away 100 sets of golf clubs, but only 30 kids actually accepted the offer. "The kids all want to grow up to be Michael Jordan," he told *Newsweek*. Earl, Tiger and others were hoping to change that situation, to make golf a more open game, and one all races could have access to at all levels.

Another reason there were so few minorities pursuing a golf career is that the game, even at the amateur level, is expensive. Tiger was grateful that his father had saved and prepared financially so that he could play. The round of amateur tournaments were very costly. Just one summer's travel and hotel expenses on the national circuit in 1991 cost the family more than $20,000. The expense, along with the opportunity for exposure to the game, has limited the number of blacks that play. "You've got to have money to play golf—that's just the way it is," Tiger says. "I'm glad my dad planned for the expenses when I was very young."[15]

THE ROAD TO VICTORY

THE TREETOPS SWAYED indifferently as the young atheletes below strained to become the next victor of the 1994 U. S. Amateur Golf Championship, held in September at the Sawgrass Stadium course in Ponte Vedra, Florida. But below on the course, the young golfers were playing as if their lives were at stake. For one competitor, though he was already well-known, it was more than a matter of another trophy.

Eldrick "Tiger" Woods, the young golfing phenomenon with a reputation for steely nerves, was playing in his very first U. S. Amateur. The competition was match play, which means the player taking the fewer number of strokes to sink the ball into any particular hole is the winner of the hole. To win the contest the player must win the most holes, regardless of the total number of strokes he takes during the round.

The Championship consisted of 36 holes; after 13 holes, Tiger found that he was six holes behind the leader. By the time 27 holes had been played, he had narrowed the gap but still had a three-hole deficit. He continued to find his birdies, and was pulling even with Trip Kuehne of Oklahoma, the leader, by the seventeenth hole.

Woods now began to create another miracle, hitting a "fearless tee shot," in the words of some spectators, on the 17th hole, a short par-3. The ball landed on the green, just four paces from the water's edge. "You don't see too many pros hit it to the right of that pin," Kuehne later recalled for the *New York Times*. "It was a great gamble that paid off."

Woods dropped a 14-foot putt and played beautifully on the 18th hole to become the youngest winner of America's oldest golf championship. He also became the first African-American champion of the event. In doing so, this exceptional athelete continued the amazing track record that he had accumulated so far in his career. He had already reigned supreme as the National Junior Amateur Champion from 1991 through 1994. Now he was simply the amateur champion, with no "junior" put before the title.

"It's an amazing feeling to come from that many down to beat a great player," said Woods of his victory. "It's indescribable."

In October of 1994 Tiger was part of the American team that attempted to capture the World Amateur

Team Championship. A total of 45 four-man teams came from all over the planet to meet in the lush French countryside, near the grandiose palace at Versailles. Tiger by now was known as the 'boy wonder', and clearly had the most crowd-gathering power of anyone on the amateur tour. But glamour would not be enough. He would have to help his mates on the U.S. team win its first World Amateur Championship in a dozen years.

The World Amateur began in 1958, when 29 countries competed for the Eisenhower Trophy at the Old Course in St. Andrews. That year Australia upset the U.S. The Americans were out for revenge two years later at the Merion course, outside Philadelphia, and won by 42 total strokes. Although the U.S. won eight of the next 11 World Amateurs, it came to Versailles with an unenviable streak of five straight runner-up finishes. The fact that the Americans lost to a different team each time spoke well of the improvement in world golf, but this year's U.S. contingent—which besides Woods included Todd Demsey, the 22-year-old 1993 NCAA champion from Arizona State, and 42-year-old John Harris, the 1993 U.S. Amateur champion—was the favorite to regain the Eisenhower Trophy.

Tiger seemed slightly disoriented due to the chilly, 38-degree morning temperature when he started out at *Golf de La Boulie*, a dense, wooded course built in 1887. His game was not his best, but after a few bogeys he turned things around for the next seven holes. His signature comeback was ready for action as he eagled the 507-yard, 17th hole with a drive, a four-iron and a 20-foot putt. Next he birdied the 18th to finish with a one-under-par 70.

The final three rounds moved to the newly designed Golf National's *L'Albatros* course, which opened in 1990, and where The French Open had been held for the previous four years. Tiger was still not quite up to his usual standard and scored a 75. That left the U.S. behind Ireland and Great Britain by one stroke for the day. "I'm putting so well, but I can't hit it," Tiger mumbled as he headed for more practice at the driving range. Tiger honed in on a slight reverse pivot after hitting a couple buckets of balls. "I'm going to be tough to beat now," he said.

The next morning Tiger was bright-eyed, and opened with birdies on the first two holes, then made three more to turn the front nine in 31 and survived two late three-putts to shoot 67, including a birdie on the last hole. Combined with steady rounds from several others, by day's end the U.S. led by one stroke over Ireland and Great Britain and four over Australia. The U.S. team won the Eisenhower Trophy once again.

There was more to Tiger's life than golf. Tida and Earl Woods had always stressed the importance of a quality education. If Tiger's golf talent ever failed, a university degree from a good school would help ensure success.

As early as junior high school, Tiger was bent on attending prestigious Stanford University, which is one of the finest universities in the country (recently chosen by presidential daughter Chelsea Clinton, who will enter as a freshman in the fall of 1997). Woods contacted Stanford golf coach Wally Goodwin, saying he had great interest in attending the school. But the young athlete would have no trouble getting past the stringent acadenic qualifications, because he was a straight-A student. He was accepted immediately, and the news became a media event.

"We heard from virtually every major media outlet in the country," recalled Gary Migdal, Assistant Athletic Director at Stanford. "News-papers, magazines, TV stations, all major networks, *Time, Newsweek, Sports Illustrated*, you name it. It was immediate and never let up."

So the 18-year-old enrolled as a freshman at Stanford, and began the normal routine of cramming for tests, getting very little sleep, and daydreaming of the future. He truly wanted to finish his degree before he turned pro. But the pressure mounted all around him to postpone college and rake in outrageous amounts of money for product endorsements. Tiger told *Sports Illustrated,* "Money won't make me happy. If I turned pro, I'd be giving up something I wanted to accomplish. And if I did turn pro, that would only put more pressure on me to play well because I would have nothing to fall back on. I would rather spend four years here at Stanford and improve myself."

Tida and Earl did not visit their son at Stanford for about six months after his arrival because they wanted him to be on his own. Tida said, "It is time for him to have his own life now." The parents who guided their son to early stardom were trusting his professors to carry on their work and bring him gently into adulthood.

It was going to be tough to keep Tiger from turning pro for four years. There were offers everywhere to lure him away from the classrooms of Stanford. Earl and Tiger were constantly receiving requests for interviews, autographs, introductions and deals. But Stanford would prove something of a refuge for Tiger. As he told *Newsweek,* "I'm not a celebrity at Stanford. Everybody's special. You have to be to get in here.

So then, nobody is. That's why I love the place."[17] Fellow freshman included actor Fred Savage of "The Wonder Years" television comedy, and gymnast Dominique Dawes, who would go on to compete in the Olympics.

Tiger settled into more-or-less normal life as a college student. He pledged the Sigma Chi Fraternity, and inbetween his studies enjoyed going to parties and other social events. He soon became known not only as a champion golfer, but as a terrible dancer. One Stanford friend, Jake Poe, remembered: "Mark this down. Tiger Woods may be the greatest golfer of all time, but he is probably the worst dancer."

He was also subject to the usual kidding of freshman by upperclassmen. Woods would take his contact lenses out at night in the dormitory, and put on thick-lensed glasses for study. The glasses were so thick that one senior began calling Woods "Urkel," after a funny-looking character on the television show "Family Matters." Tiger hated the nickname, but it stuck.

Though Woods liked the idea of being just another student, one chilling incident brought home the fact that he was Tiger Woods, the well-known golfer, and that not everyone was pleased with the idea. When he returned to his dormitory late one night, he was accosted by a knife-wielding mugger in the parking lot. "Tiger, give me your wallet," the man demanded. In danger for his life, Tiger handed over his watch to the robber, as well as a gold chain his mother had given him. The thief then used the knife butt to knock his victim to the ground, injuring his jaw in the process.

After the police were called, Woods tried to make light of the incident to his dad. But it was obvious that his high visibility and celebrity posed a possible threat of violence not only from racists or hate groups, but from others as well. Other celebrities had been injured or killed by stalkers or deranged fans. Decades before, Frank Sinatra Jr. had disappeared and been reported as kidnapped in a famous case.

Such incidents must have always worried Earl Woods; part of the reason he travelled with Tiger was to act as a lookout or one-man security force for his increasingly famous son. But in the future, real security men would be employed to keep the young golfer out of harm's way.

Apart from this incident and the delivery of one racist, hate-filled letter from an anonymous sender when Tiger was a freshman, his time at Stanford proceded in a more-or-less normal fashion.

He of course played on the Stanford golf team, and spent as much time on the practice range as he could. The area became his home away from his dormitory, Stern Hall.

"We always had a great time on the driving range," said one teammate, Eri Crum. "There was a dormitory called the Suites, and Woods's big trick was to pull out his driver and hit big slices over Suites and back onto the driving range."

Wally Goodwin, a golf coach who has been with Stanford for forty years, said ,"Tiger is the best athlete I've ever known in this sport. But he is a better kid than he is a player, and I mean that."[18]

As a member of the Stanford golf team, Tiger compiled an enviable record. Though a freshman, he won his first collegiate tournament, the William Tucker Invitational, held in Albuquerque, New Mexico. Then he went on to win the Jerry Pate Invitational Tournament. He gathered steam his second year, and finished by either winning or helping his team win in the last five events. All of this was topped off by the NCAA title for an individual golfer.

But, as pleasant as his university days were, few thought that Tiger would actually stay at Stanford for the entire four years.

The wind was filled with the sweet scent of magnolia as Tiger teed off in the first round of the 1995 Masters at Augusta, Georgia. Babyfaced

Woods was only 19 and had won more amateur tournaments than Bobby Jones and Jack Nicklaus.

Tiger was fully poised and ready for the competition. In the 61 years the Masters had been held, Woods would be only the fourth 'black' player to participate in the tournament. Lee Elder became the first black to play in the Masters in 1975, at the age of 40. Calvin Peete competed eight times but never won. Jim Thorpe played the Masters six times; but none of the black golfers ever finished in the top ten. The champion of the event is presented with a bright kelly-green blazer, which may seem garrish to many non-golfers, but to the golf enthuasist there is no higher honor.

In preparation for the Masters, Tiger had practiced putting on the polished basketball court at Stanford's Maples Pavilion. The fast, slippery greens of Augusta wouldn't be a problem for him. Tiger told *Newsweek*, "Can I do well? Doing well is winning. To walk where Jones and Nicklaus walked, that will be daunting. But I'm not afraid of the Masters. I've never been afraid of anything. I'm going down there to win."[19]

But winning isn't everything, especially when you lose. When the tournament was over, Woods had finished a respectable but distant 41st. Texas-based pro Ben Crenshaw stole the show as he earned a second green blazer. For Tiger, exposure to one of golf's toughest competitions would have to be reward enough for now.

Later in 1995, Tiger competed in the U.S. Open at the Shinnecock Hills clourse in Southampton, New York, and went on the play in the Britsh Open, held each year at St.Andrews, the historic "links" in Scotland. His appearances were disappointing. But, he was still an amateur. He was still learning.

In August, 1996, Tiger played for the last time the U. S. Amateur at Pumpkin Ridge near Portland, Oregon. He and his family had decided he should turn pro. That knowledge might have shaken the skills of another player, or decreased his desire to win. But not Tiger. Earl Woods said later, "It only made him want it more." When Tiger was asked about when he would turn pro, he merely said, "In the future." He had a chance to make history at Pumpkin Ridge; if he won, it would be for a record third straight time. But Tiger only said: "I can't afford to think about it, I know from experience that just causes anxiousness."[20]

At the U.S. Amateur, the lowest-scoring 64 players after two rounds of medal play qualify for match play. Tiger easily qualified as medalist, with a score of 69-67-136. He didn't encounter any difficulties until the championship's 18-hole semifinal. There, he was down by two after four holes to Joel Kribel, his Stanford teammate. At the 10th, he saved himself with a fabulous 50-yard approach shot from a bunker. His confidence was back, while Kribel's crumbled. Woods won the match after making two birdies and an eagle on the back nine.

The next day, Tiger was in trouble early again, going 4 down in the opening nine of the 36-hole final against Steve Scott, who had begun his sophomore year at Florida State the same week. Over 15,000 fans watched him fall into a five-hole deficit with 16 holes to play.

His trademark comeback of incredible drives and long, steady putts had to be put into action. A mistake at this point would be impossible to correct. The afternoon 18 holes showcased Scott shooting what would have been a solid two-under-par 70 in medal play. But Woods hustled up a bogeyless 65, the low round in the championship which had had 312 competitors only seven days ago. Tiger's claws were showing as he won the next three holes beginning with the 21st. He closed to within one hole, but Scott sank an outstanding shot on the 28th to go 2 up.

The next hole, a 553-yard par-5, challenged Tiger to slam a 350-yard drive and then blast a five-iron to within 45 feet of the cup. He then calmly rolled in a curling downhill putt for an eagle which overcame Scott's birdie. Scott replied with a birdie on the 32nd hole, where Tiger missed a six-foot putt to halve. With two down and only three holes left to play, Tiger sank an eight-footer for a birdie, winning the 34th hole. Flashes of frustration were traded for the will to win on the 35th hole with a long 35-foot putt which curled into the hole. As his ball dropped into the cup, Tiger waved his arm in triumph. Later he said, "That's a feeling I'll remember for the rest of my life."

But the match wasn't decided yet. The 36th was halved by the rivals, which meant that the championship would have to be decided in "sudden death," or extra, holes.

The first was full of suprises for Scott. He missed an 18-foot putt which would have won him the championship. On the 38th hole, a 194-yard par-3, Woods hit a shot that he and coach Harmon had been working on for more than a year. Tiger's gently fading six-iron landed only 12 feet from the cup. But then Tiger missed his first putt, as did Scott. The soon-to-be-pro nailed the 18-inch putt to take the lead and the championship.

Scott, though bested, showed true sportsmanship and did not wallow in defeat. He said: "That was probably the best U. S. Amateur final match ever. Just to be a part of it, I feel completely a winner."

Tiger had now gone down in the record books in the company of Bobby Jones and Jack Nicklaus as one of the greatest amateurs ever to play the game of golf.

And perhaps it was the time to turn professional, just as many in the sports media had said he would. The money that could be made was too tempting; there were rumors of a huge endorsement contract.

Tiger withdrew from Stanford the night before he would have begun his Junior year. But he promised himself and his parents that he would be back to finish his economics degree in the future.

"I had intended to stay in school, play four years at Stanford and get my degree, but things change," Tiger said. "I didn't know my game was going to progress to this point. It got much harder to get motivated for college matches, and since I accomplished my goal of winning the NCAA, it was going to get harder still. Finally, winning the third Amateur in a row is a great way to go out. I always said I would know when it was time, and now is the time."[21]

Earl told his son, "I want you to finish school because Jack Nicklaus did not finish school, Arnold Palmer did not finish school. Curtis Strange did not finish school."

Tiger said, "I promise you, Pop."

On August 28, 1996, the press had a field day as Tiger, age 20, held a press conference to announce he was trading in his bookbag for a golfbag. And close on the heels of this news an announcement that Nike, one of the largest manufacturers of sporting goods and sports apparel in the world, had signed the young man to an endorsement contract worth a reported 43 million dollars over a five-year period. The company had previously put basketball superstar Michael Jordan under contract for staggering sums. They had actively pursued Tiger for some time through his parents.

Nike's CEO, Phil Knight, was effusive with praise for Woods, and later stated: "What Michael Jordan did for basketball, [Woods] absolutely can do for golf. It's almost art." He then went on to make a comparison of Woods to Claude Monet, the 19th-century French impressionist painter.

At a press conference after he announced his pro status, Woods opened by saying charmingly,

Tiger with actor Kevin Costner at the AT&T Pebble Beach
National Pro-Am in January, 1997. (AP/Wide World Photos)

"Well, I guess it's Hello World." Later the press
corps learned that this was a tag line of the Nike ad
campaign which aired on TV two days later.

In an obvious attempt to appeal to the "minority
market" for its sports clothing line, the earliest Nike
ad showed Tiger portrayed as a victim of racism.

The words "There are still [golf] courses in the United States I am not allowed to play because of the color of my skin," appeared over film footage of Woods. And then: "I've heard I'm not ready for you. Are you ready for me?"

But not everybody was certain that Tiger was breaking new ground on the question of racial barriers. Jim Thorpe, the African-American PGA veteran, told *Sports Illustrated*: "It's more bull than Tiger. That road has been paved by the Charlie Siffords, the Lee Elders, the Calvin Peetes, the Jim Dents...With Sifford and Elder, you'd hear the "N" word, but I didn't hear it. Tiger's got it made."[22]

But there was no question the corporate world now had a hot property that, if handled right, could rake in many millions in new profits. The handsome, charming, self-confident wonder would be a huge money-maker for any product he endorsed. He eats, drinks, talks on the telephone, gets dressed, travels and plays just like the rest of the human race, and every company wanted him . It was not long before Titleist, a well-known manufacturer of golfing equipment, jumped on the loveboat and offered another huge money deal. The combined compensations from the two companies reportedly exceeded 60 million dollars. And that seemed just the beginning.

Earl Woods felt that the increased exposure

would raise his son to an almost universal level of importance. "There is no comprehension by anyone on the impact this kid is going to have, not only on the game of golf, but on the world itself," he said. "The Lord sent him here on a mission and it will transcend the game."[23] Earl had handled the endorsement negotiations, perhaps the largest bidding war ever for a young athlete.

But, Tiger would still have to play golf, and prove himself as a professional. As *Time* magazine stated, "When a kid becomes a pro, there is always the question of whether he can handle all the attention. let alone the demands of the game."

Butch Harmon, Tiger's swing coach said, "All the amateur titles Tiger has won won't mean anything, and he'll have to prove himself in a hard environment where there is no mercy. He's got the intelligence and the tools to succeed very quickly. My only worry is that he's losing two of the best years of his life to something that is very demanding for a young person. Considering everything, he's making the right decision, but he's going to have to grow up faster than I'd like him to."[24]

"THE GREAT BLACK HOPE"

THE ANNOUNCEMENT THAT Tiger Woods would be changing his rank from amateur to professional was made the day before the opening round of the Greater Milwaukee Open. When Tiger arrived at the registration desk in Milwaukee he was a little low on cash and didn't have enough to pay for his entry fee. The new multi-millionaire turned to his father and requested a loan, just as any other 20-year-old would do. Earl paid the $100 fee, and the dawning of a new era in golf had begun.

The fans anxiously awaited Tiger's debut. When he did appear, the reactions could have been for an Elvis Presley or a Michael Jordan. Tiger was recognized instantly. And he did not disappoint them. His first shot as a professional golfer was a memorable 336-yard drive straight down the center of the fairway. He shot a 67 on the first day of the Open, and followed that with a score of 69 the second day of play.

The third day of the tournament, however, Tiger started to show signs of fatigue. He scurried to pull a 73 for the day, a score that took him out of contention. On the final day of the tournament, he rallied with a 68, and thrilled the crowd with a hole-in-one, the ninth of his life, on the 188-yard 14th. As his first professional tournament came to an end, the talented young man knew that many challenges awaited him.

Tiger's immediate goal was to qualify for the 1997 PGA Tour by getting himself into the top 125 players on the 1996 earnings list. If Tiger could earn $150,000 or more in the next few months, he should make the top 125. Also, If he won a tournament he would not have to qualify for two years. If he couldn't do one or the other, it meant he would have to earn one of only 40 spots left open by playing at the PGA Tour Qualifying Tournament, something he didn't want to do.

He would have only two months to complete this mission. Following Milwaukee, Tiger had a full calendar, playing in the Canadian Open, the Quad City Classic, the B.C. Open, the Las Vegas Invitational, the Texas Open and the Disney/Oldsmobile Classic.

Loren Roberts, who had just won the Milwaukee tournament, told *Sports Illustrated:* "He's come along at exactly the right time. He's like Arnold Palmer, a guy who is going to popularize the sport to a bigger audience, to reach out to areas where maybe golf has been slow to reach . . .

A proud Tida Woods shows a headline of Tiger as he was thrilling crowds at the Asian Honda Classic, held in her native Thailand. (AP/Wide World Photos)

There's no question he is going to do well. When you hit your best shot and look up and he's 60 yards in front of you, that's impressive, to start. But he's still going to have to beat those 156 other guys out here. That's not going to be as easy as some people think."[25]

Others pros thought that Tiger had just gotten

started. "I played with him on his bad day, nothing working for him, and I was impressed," reported veteran Bruce Lietzke to *Sports Illustrated.* " You learn about somebody when he's having that kind of day. A lot of 20-year-olds would get frustrated, angry. He never lost his temper, still kept working. If he's going to be the game's next great ambassador, then the game is in good hands."

The tour was beginning to take its toll on Tiger after five weeks, as he declined to participate in the Buick Challenge in Pine Mountain, Georgia. He was exhausted, both physically and mentally, and needed a break. Many of his fellow players criticized him for withdrawing from the tournament, saying that he still had a lot to learn. They were disappointed that Tiger didn't just play through the pressure and follow their rules.

Top pro Davis Love III spoke for many of the older golfers when he said, "I guess once he made his money [from endorsements], it's got to be a letdown. But withdrawing on Wednesday, well, he's a rookie. He'll learn. You've got to play by the rules." Curtis Strange added, "This tournament was one of seven to help him out at the beginning with sponsor exemptions when he needed help, and how quickly he forgot."

Tiger's fifth start as a pro was The Las Vegas Invitational, held from October 2-6 at the Las Vegas Country Club. He was playing well, but after three rounds was trailing his playing partner Davis Love III by three strokes. He scored a final-round 64 to send the tournament into a sudden-death playoff with Love. And here, Woods' match-play experience came to the fore. When the first extra hole was finished, Tiger had achieved his first tournament win. During the five-day event, Tiger's scores were 70-63-68-67-64—332. Earnings from his victory were $297,000.

Two weeks later, Tiger played at The Walt Disney World/Oldsmobile Classic, held October 17-20 at Walt Disney World, Orlando, Florida. He was now protected by a posse of four bodyguards. Attendance had tripled from the year before at The Disney, who were deleriously happy to have the young pro compete there. It was reported that the tournament director had actually jumped into a swimming pool from sheer joy when he learned that Tiger would be playing at their tournament.

Again, Tiger played well. The final day of The Disney, Tiger was tied with Payne Stewart. Stewart was tough, but Woods was tougher still as he

Part of the reception for Tiger during the Honda Classic was this "welcome home" party. Here Woods and his caddy Mike Cowan attempt to learn a traditional Thai dance from a pretty lady. (AP/Wide World Photos)

blasted a 66 to finish ahead of Stewart's 67 and win the tournament.

The Disney was Tiger's second win out of seven starts, and no player had had a start like that since Curtis Strange, 14 years earlier. Tiger was considered a rookie with the Tour, but he certainly was playing like an old pro.

Tiger also now held the 23rd rank in earnings for the year, and had won a pole position at the hallowed Tour Championship at Southern Hills in Tulsa. Although he had already sent in his $3,000 entry fee for the PGA Tour Qualifying Tournament in December, he wouldn't be needing to qualify.

He had already secured a qualification.

The Nike-clad kid would bring the faithful fans to Tulsa too. Some would be on a golf course for the very first time. The plush greens squeaked beneath the sneakers of the young man with his hat on backwards as he made his way around the beautifully groomed course. He seemed to be enjoying himself. Tiger would throw balls to the kids in the audience as he passed by or while he was preparing to slam another 300-yard drive. The young ladies were also anxious to get a glimpse of the handsome young golfer as he walked across the green.

The course at Southern Hills in Tulsa was not one to favor Woods's game; thick trees and heavy rough along with the narrow fairways limited his abilities. He played a good first round, but not a great one. Tiger told *The New York Times,* "I'm very satisfied, you shoot 70 around here, that's pretty good, no matter what the conditions are . . . The first round I just want to get off to a good start so you don't blow yourself out of the tournament"[26]

But that beautiful day would change into a frightening evening. Tiger spent most of the night before the second round with his father. Earl had been hospitalized with chest pains he suffered around 2 a.m. The cause of the chest pains were related to bronchial problems, and he was admitted to St. Francis Hospital in Tulsa.

Tiger stayed at the hospital with Earl until 5 a.m., and then tried to sleep for a few hours before returning to the course. But he teed off shakily and could not concentrate because he was so concerned about his father. The result was the worst round since he turned pro. Tida arrived at the course by the time Tiger had reached the third hole. He had double-bogeyed the second hole after hooking his drive into a water hazard. Tida said, "It's obvious he's not concentrating."

Earl was feeling well enough to request a television so that he could watch the tournament, as Tida left him to go comfort Tiger. A hospital spokesman reported that there was fluid at the base of Earl's left lung, but that his condition was not considered serious.

Tiger's score was 43 on the front nine, but he soon turned it around on the back nine, shooting an even-par 35. He greatly impressed a fellow competitor, John Cook, who did not know about Tiger's dad until they were on the 10th hole. "He showed me a lot today, and it wasn't golf," Cook told *The New York Times*. "You can lose your mind out there and he didn't. He didn't put his head down and sulk. He just tried to fight through it."

Tiger's sleep-weary score of 78 knocked him out of contention for the $3 million prize. But his mind was on his father, not golf. He said of his father, "Hopefully he's O.K., I'm going to see him right now. I didn't want to be here today, because there are more important things in life than golf. I love my dad to death and I wouldn't want to see anything happen to him."

Earl had undergone coronary bypass surgery 10 years earlier, and the hospital continued to observe him and to conduct more tests. By the next afternoon he had shown great improvement.

Tiger made an appearance when Kelli Kuehne, a good friend and the sister of former competitor Trip Kuehne, was making her professional golf debut at the December 1996 J.C. Penney Classic. Paired in a mixed-team match with Kuehne, Tiger offered her several pieces of advice as they played together. His advice on crowd control included, "It sounds kind of simple, but you've got to keep moving. You sign as you go, keeping one eye on where you're going. If you are here, and you stop, you will never get there."

The two made a cute couple. But with back-to-back U.S. Amateur titles to go alongside good looks and an endorsement contract with Nike, the 19-year-old Kuehne was hardly taking the side door into her pro career. Kuehne kept her game in good enough shape to finish tied for second in her initial event. "There was so much added pressure being Tiger's partner," LPGA veteran Donna Andrews said. "It was a hard spot to be in with all the attention."

No one questioned the real friendship of the two young golfers, but the famous Nike 'swoosh' logo was much in evidence, on golf caps, shirts, golf bags. It looked to be not so much an event as a photo-opportunity, pairing the young prince of golf with a young princess.

Things had certainly changed for Tiger since the days when he was still an amateur and a student. Tiger defended his past showings against professionals: "You guys don't understand, when I played in those tournaments, I was either in high school or college. I'd get dumped into the toughest places to play, and I usually was trying to study, get papers done and everything else. I knew if I came out here and played every day, I'd get into a rhythm, and I have." [84]

Though known for his long drives and distance shots, the rest of Tiger's game was improving. At the B.C. Open, he told *The New York Times,* "My short game is the best part of my game, I'm not the greatest of ball-strikers, but I can get up and down from a lot of places. My short game gives me the ability to salvage rounds. It's nice when you don't have it and you're still in contention. Look at the hallmark of all the great players, especially Nicklaus. They had the ability to turn a 72 or 73 into a 67 or 68."

Tiger's scoring average as a pro was 67.89, but he did not have enough rounds under his belt in 1996 to qualify for the Vardon Trophy, given each year to the pro with the lowest average for each 18 holes played. His impressive statistics in other areas left most of the competition behind. Tiger's driving range of 302.8 was 14 yards better than second-place John Daly's. He averaged 4.68 birdies per round, and his eagle frequency was one out of every 55 holes.

Still, the young phenomenon thought he could improve. As he told *Sports Illustrated,* "I really haven't played my best golf yet, I haven't even had a great putting week yet."

For his fast start as a professional, Woods was named 1996 Rookie of the Year by the Professional Golfers Association. He finished 24th on the money list with prize winnings of $790,594. This was the second-highest total for a rookie in Tour history, and was accomplished in only eight tournaments.

Tiger's 1997 Tour began at The Mercedes Championships, held January 9-12 at La Costa Resort and Spa in Carlsbad, California. Tiger's scores in the abbreviated event—the final round was washed out by rain—were 70-67-65—202, which tied him for the lead with the reigning Player of the Year, Tom Lehman. The sudden-death playoff only lasted one hole as Lehman sent his drive on the par-3, 7th hole into a water hazard. Tiger placed his shot within a few feet of the hole, and sank the easy putt for another victory.

Of Wood's play that day, veteran Tom Watson, who won 33 PGA tournaments and is considered the only really great player since Nicklaus, said this: "It's his attitude. He has this attitude where he wants to win every tournament. That's very unique these days . . . You have to learn to play just to beat people's butts. . . I think Tiger has proven that he can do that."

By now, there was no doubt that Tiger Woods could win professional golf tournaments. Doubtless, he had the ability to be a truly great golfer, perhaps to dominate the sport. But he had not won a major championship as a pro. His play had sometimes been sparkling, at other times erratic. The Masters tournament was coming in the Spring. Many African-American and other fans hoped he could win, to prove that a 'black' player could beat the best, when it really counted. Some magazines and newspapers had tagged him "The Great Black Hope."

The racial issue cut both ways, however. Just as Tiger had occasionally been ostracized for being black, he had also sometimes been criticized by the African-American community for not being 'black' enough; Some felt that he had not been a strong enough advocate for continued advancement in civil rights. African-Americans had even picketed Woods for playing in a tournament at Shoal Creek, a Birmingham club which in its history had discriminated against blacks. (In 1990 the founder of Shoal Creek Country Club told a reporter that there wasn't any way that an African-American would ever be considered for membership. The PGA Championship was announced to be held at Shoal Creek, and the rules changed quickly and dramatically.)

The policy makers of golf had, in recent years, made a strong effort to amend their rules to reflect that any club with restrictive membership policies could not host a tournament event. It has been the beginning of a new era in the traditionally all-white sport.

For his part, Tiger didn't want to be a crusader. He simply said again, "I don't want to be the best black golfer ever, I want to be the best *golfer* ever."

But perhaps the criticism had struck a nerve. Announced in January was the formation by Woods and his parents of the Tiger Woods Foundation to promote golf and non-sports activities for disadvantaged children.

"Golf for inner-city youth has increased," Tiger said. "But it isn't what it should be. We need to focus on the problems. I have a chance to make a big impact."

Woods planned to run six golf clinics for children during the week preceding PGA events in

Orlando, Fla.; Dallas; New York and Chicago; as well as tentatively in Miami and Memphis, Tenn.

Earl Woods stated that the foundation was concerned with more than golf. "We're interested in the total kid," he said in a statement. "Our goal is to make these youngsters better people." And, he added, the effort would not be confined by national boundaries: "The Tiger is not limited to America. He's a citizen of the world."

Tiger makes a face after something unusual for him, a bad shot. (AP/Wide World Photos)

THE MASTERS, AND BEYOND

AS THE MASTER'S Tournament approached, Tiger Woods must have felt the pressure building. He had, as an amateur, played six tournament rounds at the legendary Augusta National course, but had yet to break par. However, some experts were making a bet that the young golfer had a good chance to win the prestigious tourament, in fact that he was actually the favorite. *Sports Illustrated* had earlier in the year predicted that Woods would win. Las Vegas gambling odds-makers had also chosen him as one of the favorites, although right behind Nick Faldo, who had won the tournament three times, and the great Australian golfer, Greg Norman.

Nick Faldo was one doubter. Though he admired Woods' exceptional talent, he felt it would take a more seasoned player to handle the pressure and the demanding course in the Master's. "I think there's a learning curve of playing Augusta and the discipline of playing the golf course," Faldo said of Woods. "When to hit the ball. When not. When to make that par and walk. It's not impossible, but I think experience does help here."

Woods had his own counter for that. "I guess being here for the third time, it definitely does change the aura of the place," the young golfer said. "Because you're accustomed to it, you know what to expect." Then he added, "I just came here to win. That's what I'm going to do in every tournament."

Golf legends Jack Nicklaus and Arnold Palmer thought that Woods had an excellent chance. Palmer stated, "I don't think that there is anything to stop him from winning right here or anywhere else." Jack Nicklaus had earlier made a prediction that Woods probably would win as many Master's tournaments as he had (six) and as had Palmer (four) put together.

Woods, for his part, had confidence but showed some modesty. "Whether I will [win], I don't know. Only time will tell...there's definitely a chance that my game is such that it suits this golf course, and maybe one day I might do that."

Those who favored Woods cited the Augusta course as being particularly long, favoring golfers who could hit mighty tee shots; also, there was little rough or out of bounds areas, so that an errant tee shot slightly off course would not be a problem. However, perhaps Woods' short game would be the key. He was capable of stroking in 30 and 40 foot putts on occasion, but was also capable of the

Woods embraces his father after the Masters victory. (AP/Wide World)

erratic shot on the green, sometimes missing short putts when his concentration was not at its best. However, he was going into the tournament on a roll. In a practice match at his home course in Orlando, he had just the week before shot a 59, a most remarkable score even for Woods, and the best round he had ever played.

During the second week of April, 1997, history was made at The Masters Tournament in Augusta, Georgia. He indeed had been ready for the tournament, firing a 70 the first day, and following with very low rounds of 66 and 65. By the last day, Sunday, he was far in the lead. Pro Tom Watson said, "the only remining question is second place."

Wood's long drives were equaled by his consistency with approach shots, and a sure hand with his putter. His only bogey came on the 7th hole; after that, he was consistent, playing up to his own high standards. His match play experience helped him handle any remaining nerves he might have had, and as he went into the final nine holes, his lead only increased over Tom Kite, the nearest rival. As he walked up the 18th hole, he waved his hat to the gallery, smiling broadly.

Tida Woods was right behing her son, walking the entire 18 holes as a spectator. And when he holed in his last short putt for the victory, Earl Woods was waiting for him. The two exchanged a long embrace.

It was the culmination—or perhaps the start—of a long road of hope and final victory.

When Tiger slipped into the traditional green

blazer, the symbol of victory (in Tiger's case, a size 42-long), perhaps it did herald a new era in the sport of professional golf. There has never been such an astounding performance at The Masters Tournament. Tiger now holds the record for the lowest score ever at 270; the largest point margin of victory at 12 (eclipsing the record set by his idol Jack Nicklaus); and a record total score of 18-under-par, bettering Nicklaus' previous record of 271 in 1965 by one stroke (Raymond Floyd had tied the Nicklaus record in 1976). Tiger, at 21 years old, was also the youngest player ever to win the Masters, as well as the first person of color.

Woods' day was made complete by a congratulatory phone call from President Bill Clinton. Tiger, perhaps realizing for the first time how important his victory might be as a social statement, said: "Winning here will do a lot for the game of golf. I am in a unique position because a lot of kids look up to me as a role model."

Television ratings for the Masters Tournament were also at a record level. The television sets in more than 8 million homes were attuned to the CBS channel for the last day.

Bryant Gumbel, the black CBS news commentator, had this to say: "The way he played and conducted himself was absolutely exceptional . . . It is another crack in the armor of those people who want to say African-Americans are incapable of doing this or that. I am applauding loudly."

Woods was magnanimous in victory, citing those black golfing pioneers who had come before him. "I wasn't the pioneer," Woods elaborated. "Charlie Sifford, Lee Elder, Ted Rhodes, those are the guys who paved the way . . . Coming up 18, I said a little prayer of thanks to those guys. Those guys are the ones who did it." Elder, who had driven to the tournament from his home in Fort Lauderdale, Florida, had been waiting in the crowd beyond the 18th green. He had this to say: "I am so proud we have a black champion. That's going to have major significance. It will open the door for more blacks to become members here. It will get more minority kids involved in golf."

An incident with racial overtones was to remind everyone that, though Woods was now the champion and the "color barrier" had been broken at Augusta, there was still much to do to make golf colorblind.

Fuzzy Zoeller, a popular pro (and, ironically, the only other golfer to win at Augusta his first try as a professional, in 1979) made some unfortunate and disparaging comments to a film crew on the last day of the tournament. He referred several times to Woods as a "little boy" and wondered aloud whether Woods would choose "fried chicken and collard greens, or whatever the hell they serve"[29] at the champion's banquet in 1998.

Zoeller later made a public apology after drawing criticism from the media and the National Association for the Advancement of Colored People. He also made an emotional statement before withdrawing from the Greater Greensboro Chrysler Classic, on April 23. The apology was accepted by North Carolina NAACP acting president Skip Alston, and four days later by Woods himself, but not before the K-Mart Corporation had cancelled Zoeller's endorsment contract for a line of sporting goods sold in their stores.

Several weeks later, Zoeller and Woods would meet in person at the Mastercard Colonial Golf Tournament in Fort Worth, Texas. The meeting was cordial, though Tiger still clearly regarded Zoeller's remarks as racial rather than as a joke. There was more controversy when it was reported that some of the other pros had not appreciated Tiger's handling of the situation, thinking he should have accepted Zoeller's apology right away, rather than waiting four days and further damaging the affable pro's career. Asked if there was

Tiger, in green victory blazer, is congratulated after his win by 1996 Masters champ Nick Faldo. (AP/Wide World Photos)

resentment against him, Woods said: "I wouldn't say resentment. They just questioned it. I just told them I was brought into it, I didn't start it. I just want to play golf."[30]

And play golf he did. In mid-May, Tiger returned to regular competition and won the GTE Byron Nelson Classic in Irving, Texas, tying the tournament record with a final score of 17-under par 263. His final round was a 68. This was remarkable if for no other reason than the composure it must have taken to play the last holes amid the huge throng which crowded around, estimated at almost 100,000.

Tiger, by the end of May, had won over $1,360,000 as prize money during 1997, and was the leading money-earner on the Tour.

Shortly after the Byron Nelson victory, Tiger penned another endorsement deal, this time with the American Express Company. He will be a spokesperson for the company for five years, and compensated royally. The trade magazine *Brandweek* reported Wood's fee at $30 million for signing the contract. American Express CEO Kenneth Chenault said his company had paid the huge amount because Tiger's achievements "reflect discipline, hard work and preparation."

No one could argue with that. And it was now

certainly true that, as one magazine suggested, Tiger Woods was "the world's most famous 21-year old".

When the money, the controversy, and the instant fame have been set aside, one clear fact remains. With the Masters victory, Woods has joined the list of black "firsts" in athletics such as Arthur Ashe, the first black tennis player to win the men's division at Wimbledon, and even the great Jackie Robinson; Woods' victory came the same day a 50th-anniversary celebration of Robinson's ascension to the major leagues was celebrated in New York City. Woods was asked to attend by no less a personage than President Bill Clinton, but declined, citing exhaustion and the need for time to himself after his victory.

There were also even-more-distant echoes of Jack Johnson, the controversial heavyweight boxing champion during the first decade of this century. A more suitable comparison might be Joe Louis, long-time heavyweight champion in the 1930's and 40's, who was universally admired by all races for his soft-spoken and easy-going personality.

But, before such comparisons can be fairly

made, these things have to be noted. Though Wood's Masters victory is certainly a first and a breakthrough, the actual long-term social significance may have been over-magnified. Woods has never really had to struggle because of his race, and has never had to "wait in line" as did Robinson, baseball pitcher Satchel Paige, and other early African-American pioneers in athletics. He grew up in relatively affluent surroundings and has had the benefit of the best coaches and tutors since he was a child. His Masters purse of $486,000 is in itself a small fortune. He had earned many millions of dollars in endorsement contracts before he was 21 years old.

Some critics have suggested that the predominance of black role models in sports and entertainment is in itself harmful, particularly with respect to poor minority youngsters, and especially those growing up in inner cities. More suitable role models, it is suggested, would be the many black professionals who have done well in school and worked hard over many years to achieve a solid but less spectacular success. It is only a very few youngsters who will ever play basketball for the NBA, or for that matter walk down the 18th fairway at Augusta.

Some golfing analaysts, though at first welcoming Woods, feel that he may actually be harmful to golf in the long run. Nicklaus and Palmer were also phenomenal winners, but in that era there were other great names such as Gary Player and Lee Trevino, who on any given day could pose the strongest of challenges. Professional golf of today has needed an easily-recognizable name, someone the fans and the television audiences would pay to see. But it might be that Woods is so good, so early, that on his best days he will have no competition at all. And golf, a slow-paced sport at best, badly needs intense competition to make the last round and the last few holes of any tournament worth watching.

Some skeptics might say that Woods could be more easily likened to an Olga Korbut, or a Nadia Comaneci, Soviet-bloc Olympic Gold Medal winners in gymnastics whose entire lives from a very early age had been given over to the relentless pursuit of excellence by their parents and coaches, so that in effect they were little more than athletic machines. But, unlike the gymnasts, whose careers were over by age 20, Tiger will have many years to play competitive golf. Perhaps the real question is whether Woods will be able to have a relatively normal private and personal life off the course.

But, for the time being, he is on top of the world, liked and applauded by everyone. No one doubts his appeal as the All-American Young Man. By all accounts, he is a genuinely nice guy; It will be wonderful if he can stay that way.

Tiger realizes the effect he is having on the sport, and is pleased to see more minorities in the gallery. Young fans might call out "Go, Ti!" or scream loudly just to get a nod from him. They all love Tiger, and he loves them as well. To see more kids wanting to learn about golf, which is Tiger's life, is a dream come true for him. Some day the game may be filled with minorities, and the days when he was considered a rarity will be long gone. Brilliance comes in all colors.

Many of the players on tour think that Tiger is the most wonderful thing to happen to golf in a long, long time and look forward to watching what develops in the new era where it looks like Tiger will rule. He remains the single most powerful personality to come onto the golfing scene for many years, and his many fans will be on the edge of their seats waiting for the next tournament.

At 21, Tiger has already changed the history of sports with his attitude, grace and determination. He should be commended for his talent, his giving nature, and his early fulfillment as a role model for children. He is on a mission, and will be a huge influence for many years to come.

"I don't consider myself a Great Black Hope," Tiger has said. "I'm just a golfer who happens to be black and Asian. It doesn't matter whether you're white, black, brown or green. All that matters is I touch kids the way I can through clinics, and they benefit from them."

The kids in the gallery are the future of the game, and Tiger is the ambassador to show them the way.

Tiger Woods Chronology

(**Age of**) 10 months— Received first sawed-off club.

2— Appeared on CBS Network News.

3— Shot a score of48 for 9 holes on Navy Golf Course.
Banned from Navy Golf Course for being underage.
Appeared as a guest on "The Mike Douglas Show" with
comedian Bob Hope.

4— Entered and won first local tournament.
Put under tutelage of teaching pro Rudy Duran.

5— Appeared on TV's "That's Incredible".

8— Won Optimist International Junior World.

10— Begins lessons under John Anselmo.

12— First national competition (Big I tournament).

13— Finished second in The Insurance Youth Golf
Classic.
Recorded fifth hole-in-one.

14— Semifinalist at 1990 U.S. Junior.
Chosen as Southern California Player of the Year.
Finished second in PGA National Junior
    Championship.
Enlisted sports psychologist Jay Brunza.

15— Won 1991 U.S. Junior Amateur (youngest champ
ever).
Won Optimist International Junior World (sixth time).
Played in first U.S. Amateur.

16— Top-32 finish in 1992 U.S. Amateur.
Youngest player ever in a PGA Tour event (L.A. Open).
Won 1992 U.S. Junior (record second title).
AJGA Player of the Year.
Began working under swing coach Butch Harmon.

17— Won 1993 U.S. Junior (third straight).
Top-32 finish at 1993 U.S. Amateur.
First-Team Rolex Junior All-American (fourth consec-
    utive year).

18— Member of winning U.S. team at World Amateur
    Championships in Versailles, France.
Entered Stanford University.
GolfWorld's Man of the Year.
Won 1994 U.S. Amateur (youngest champion ever).
Competed for United States in Walker Cup in
    Porthcawl, Wales.
Won Western Amateur Championship.

19— Won collegiate debut (Tucker Invitational, Albu-
    querque, N.M.)
Won Silver medal at his first Masters for finishing as
    the low amateur.
Named Pac-10 Player of the Year.
Won 1995 U.S. Amateur (second straight).

20— Won NCAA individual title.
Named Rolex College Player of the Year.
Competed in the British Open.
Won 1996 U.S. Amateur (record third straight).
Left Stanford and turned professional.
Signed $60 million endorsement deals with Nike,
    Titleist.
Played in first tournament as a professional, the Greater
    Milwaukee Open.
Won first PGA Tournament, Las Vegas Invitational.
Won Walt Disney World/Oldsmobile Classic.

21— Selected as 1996 PGA Rookie of the Year.
Won 1997 Mercedes Championships.
Co-founded Tiger Woods Foundation.
Won Masters Tournament.
Set record as fastest PGA player to go over $1 million
    (did it in nine events; record was 27 by Ernie Els).
Won GTE Byron Nelson Classic.
Signed endorsement deal with American Express.
Became PGA Tour money leader.

Bibliography

Book:

Woods, Earl (foreword by Tiger Woods), *Training A Tiger: A Father's Guide to Raising a Winner in Both Golf and Life* (New York: HarperCollins, 1997).

Periodicals:

Ebony, May, 1995
Golf, February, 1992; July, 1995
Jet, September 11, 1995
Newsweek, April 10, 1995; September 9, 1996
People, September 16, 1996
Sports Illustrated, August 9, 1993; October 17, 1994; September 5, 1994; March 27, 1995; September 4, 1995; September 2, 1996; September 9, 1996; October 28, 1996
The New York Times, October 15-17, 1996; October 24-26, 1996; April 11, 1995
Time, September 9, 1996
T.V. Guide, October 12-18, 1996

Newsmakers 95
Greensboro Daily News, April 8-13, 1997; April 15-17, 1997; May 19-21, 1997.

GLOSSARY

Birdie: a score of one under par on a particular hole.

Bogey: a score of one stoke over par on a particular hole. A *double bogey* is a score of two strokes over par on a particular hole.

Bunker: large depressed areas, usually near the green, which are filled with sand, and serve as obstacles the golfer must avoid. Also known as a *sand trap*. A bunker is classed as a *hazard*; other hazards may be lakes or ponds, known as *water hazards*, fences, trees, etc.

Caddie: an attendant on the golf course who usually carries the golf bag and clubs for the player. Once an integral feature of the game, they have now largely been replaced by golf carts and buggies.

Clubs: the equipment used to strike the golf ball. A standard set of 14 golf clubs is divided into two types, the *woods* and the *irons*.

Course: the field on which golf is played., usually divided into 18 *holes*, or sections. The lengths of individual holes vary, as does the number of strokes needed for par.

Drive: a long shot made from the tee onto the fairway, or in the case of a par-3 hole, onto or near the green.

Eagle: a score of two under par on a particular hole. A *double eagle* is a score of three strokes less than par on a particular hole. This is only possible on a par-5 hole.

Fade: a drive or shot that flies straight but then veers gently to one direction as it approaches the green; used primarily to avoid obstacles between the golfer and the green.

Fairway: in area, the largest part of the golf course, onto which a drive is hit fron the tee.

Green: a rounded or elliptical area of closely cut grass surrounding the *cup* or *hole*. Once on the green, the player proceeds to *putt* the ball toward and into the hole.

Hole: a cup imbedded in the ground on the surface of the green. A hole is not finished until the golfer strokes the ball into the hole.

Hole-in-one: A rare feat, when a player drives the ball from the tee into the cup with one stroke.

Hook: a drive or shot that, after being hit by a right handed golfer, veers to the left. (When hit by a left-handed golfer, to the right.)

Irons: A club with a face or head made of steel or other metal. A set of irons is numbered 1 through 9, depending on the angle of the club face. A higher numbered club gives more loft to the ball than a lower numbered club.

Usually included with the irons are the *sand wedge* and the *pitching wedge,* used for approach shots to the green.

Lie: The position of the ball after it has landed.

Match Play: head-to-head competition in which two players compete, one against the other. The player who takes the least strokes on any particular hole wins the hole. The contest is won by the player or team that wins the most holes.

In *medal play* the team or player taking the least

number of strokes over the total number of holes wins.

Par: the number of strokes a player should use to comple a certain hole; also, the number of strokes a player should use to complete a round of 18 holes. Par for most 18-hole courses is 72. For individual holes, the par might be three, four, or five, depending on the length or difficulty.

Putt: a tap or gentle stroke applied to the golf ball on the green.

Putter: an iron with a flat head or face used for putting.

Rough: areas of long or thick grass, dirt or sand which border the fairway. A drive landing in the rough is more difficult to strike on the next shot.

Slice: a drive or shot that, after being hit by a right handed golfer, veers to the right. (When hit by a left-handed golfer, to the left.)

Tee: a level area, generally raised slightly above the surrounding terrain, which is the starting point of the hole. *Also*: a small peg on which the golf ball is placed for a drive or tee shot.

Woods: A set of different clubs used for driving the ball long distances, usually from the tee. The club heads were originally all made of wood, hence the name. Also known as a *driver*.

NOTES

1. Golf Magazine, February, 1992, Vol. 34, pp. 63-65.
2. Training a Tiger: A Father's Guide to Raising a Winner in Both Golf and Life, by Earl Woods with Pete McDaniel (New York: Harper Collins, 1997), p. 156.
3. Ibid., p. 170.
4. Golf Magazine, February, 1992, Vol. 34, pp. 63-65.
5. Training a Tiger, p. 180.
6. Ibid.
7. Tiger Woods, Beckett Profiles # 6, 1997.
8. Sports Illustrated, August 9, 1993, Vol. 79, pp. 58-59.
9. Ibid.
10. Ibid.
11. Sports Illustrated, March 27, 1995, Vol. 82, pp. 62-72.
12. Ibid.
13. Ibid.
14. Ibid.
15. Golf Magazine, February, 1992, Vol. 34, pp. 63-65.
16. Sports Illustrated, March 27, 1995, Vol. 62, pp. 62-72.
17. Newsweek, April 10, 1995, Vol. 1125, pp. 70-72.
18. People Weekly, September 16, 1996, Vol. 46, pp. 60-62.
19. Newsweek, April 10, 1995, Vol. 125, pp. 70-72.
20. Sports Illustrated, September 2, 1996, Vol. 85, pp. 22-
21. Ibid.
22. T.V. Guide, October 12-18, 1996, Vol. 44, p. 41.
23. Newsweek, September 9, 1996, Vol. 128, pp. 58-59.
24. Sports Illustrated, September 2, 1996, Vol. 85, pp. 22-26.
25. Sports Illustrated, September 9, 1996, Vol. 85, pp. 64-65.
26. The New York Times, October 25, 1996, B:13.

27. Sports Illustrated, October 28, 1996, Vol. 85, pp. 46-48.

28. Ibid.

29. *Greensboro Daily News*, April 8-13, 1997; April 15-17, 1997; May 19-21, 1997.

30. Ibid.

INDEX

8/03 .   12   3/03
  6/06   13   4/05
8/10   14   2/09